# BUILD YOUR OWN CRAZY CAR BOT

## Tucker Besel

BLACK RABBIT BOOKS

Hi Jinx is published by Black Rabbit Books
P.O. Box 3263, Mankato, Minnesota, 56002.
www.blackrabbitbooks.com
Copyright © 2018 Black Rabbit Books

Jennifer Besel, editor; Michael Sellner, designer;
Omay Ayres, photo researcher

Library of Congress Cataloging-in-Publication Data
Names: Besel, Tucker, author.
Title: Build your own crazy car bot /
by Tucker Besel.
Description: Mankato, Minnesota :
Black Rabbit Books, [2018] | Series: Hi jinx.
Bot maker | Audience: Age 9-12. | Audience:
Grade 4 to 6. | Includes
bibliographical references and index.
Identifiers: LCCN 2017009963 (print) |
LCCN 2017037520 (ebook) | ISBN 9781680723526
(e-book) | ISBN 9781680723229 (library binding)
| ISBN 9781680726466 (paperback)
Subjects: LCSH: Mobile robots—Design and
construction—Juvenile literature.| Automobiles—
Models—Juvenile literature.
Classification: LCC TJ211.415 (ebook) | LCC TJ211.415 .B47 2018
(print) | DDC 629.8/932—dc23
LC record available at https://lccn.loc.gov/2017009963

Printed in the United States. 10/17

## Image Credits

Grant Gould, all robot illustrations
Alamy: age fotostock, 20 (r); Dreamstime: Simm49, 5 (alligator clip); Newscom: Feature Photo Service, 20 (l); Shutterstock: 7th Son Studio, 5 (connector); aarrows, 1 (tire prints); advent, 19 (kid); AlexLMX, 5 (battery); Art'nLera, 3, 12, 16, 21 (bkdg); ARTFULLY PHOTOGRAPHER, Cover, 2-3 (glasses); belka_35, 5 (scissors); Big Boy, Cover (insects); Bill Fehr, 5, 16 (screwdriver); Bplanet, 5 (motor); braingraph, 15, 21 (robot); Christopher Hall, 15 (notes); Dualororua, 8 (grasshopper); Fedorov Oleksiy, 5 (pencil); Fleur_de_papier, 18 (tape); Galyna G, Cover, Back Cover, 1, 5, 7, 8, 11, 15, 16, 18-19 (bkgd); GreenStockCreative, 17 (eraser); The Helena, 18, 22 (lady bug); hermandesign2015, 18, 22 (bee); hoomoo, 5, 6 (pliers); iceink, 5, 9, 10 (glue gun); Ilya Chalyuk, 3, 4, 6, 20 (marker strokes); Image Wizard, Cover, 2-3 (cap); Jumnong, 5 (tape); La Gorda, 5 (bottle); mexrix, 5 (ball); Nosopyrik, 5 (ruler); opicobello, Cover, 9, 12 (highlighter); Pasko Maksim, Back Cover, 9, 15, 23, 24 (torn paper); phipatbig, 16 (arrow); PILart, 10 (splash); Pitju, 3, 16, 21 (curled paper); Pixel Embargo, 10, 17 (pencil); Rohit Dhanaji Shinde, Cover, 2–3, 10, 17, 19, 22 (ant); Rvector, Cover (steering wheel); S K Chavan, 18 (cone); tankist276, 5 (goggles); Teguh Mujiono, Cover, 8, 11, 12, 18, 19, 22 (ladybug, cricket & firefly); Thomas Bethge, 5 (craft stick); totallypic, 6-8, 10, 12-17 (arrows); Tueris, 1, 4 (marker stains); valkoinen, 5 (toothpick) Every effort has been made to contact copyright holders for material reproduced in this book. Any omissions will be rectified in subsequent printings if notice is given to the publisher.

# CONTENTS

# Chapter 1
# BE A BOT MAKER

Robots aren't just in stories. People are creating robots that walk, run, and battle. Even beginners can create bots that jump and wiggle.

This book will help you create a simple crazy car bot. Robot building takes patience. Don't give up if something isn't working. Experiment until it does. And, most importantly, have fun!

# WHAT YOU'LL NEED

ruler

scissors

electrical tape

sharpened pencil

2 4½-inch- (11-cm-)
long wood craft sticks

large eraser

safety glasses

toothpick

1¼-inch (3-cm)
alligator clip

pliers

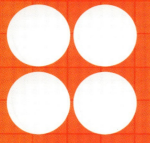
4 table tennis balls

Phillips screwdriver

9-volt battery

9-volt battery
snap connector
(with ½ inch [1 cm]
of wire exposed)

hot glue gun
and hot glue

1 plastic water
bottle with cap

2 6-volt toy motors with wires
(with ½ inch [1 cm] of wire exposed)

# Chapter 2

# LET'S BUILD!

**1.** Attach the alligator clip to the black wire of one motor. To do this, put the wire between the tabs on the back of the clip. Then use pliers to pinch the tabs together.

alligator clip

motor

pinch here

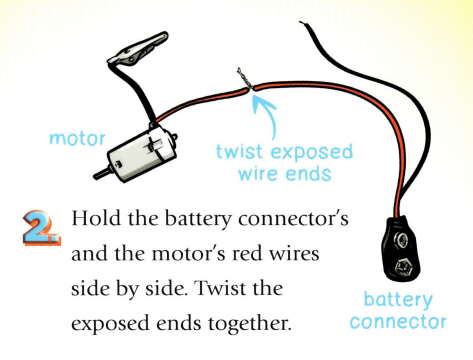

motor

twist exposed
wire ends

battery
connector

**2.** Hold the battery connector's and the motor's red wires side by side. Twist the exposed ends together.

**3.** Snap a battery into the connector. **Clamp** the alligator clip to the connector's exposed black wire. The **shaft** of the motor should spin. Unclamp the clip. Unsnap the battery.

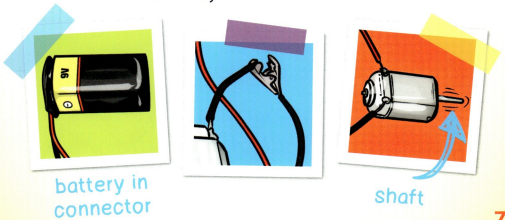

battery in
connector

shaft

**4.** Bend the twisted wire ends down. Wrap the exposed wires to the red wire with electrical tape.

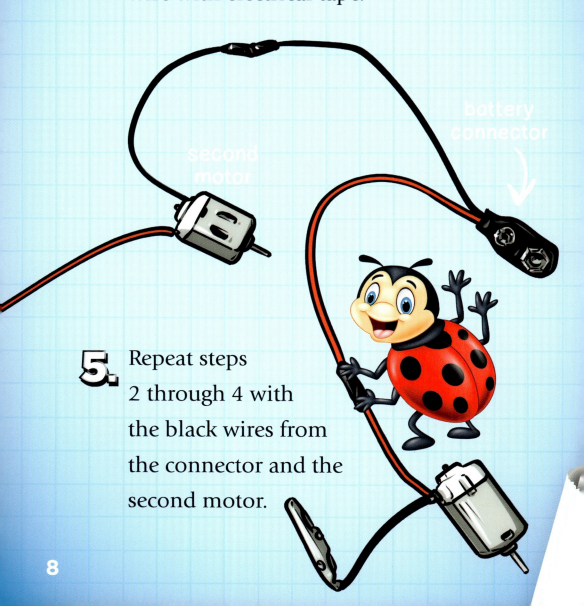

battery connector

second motor

**5.** Repeat steps 2 through 4 with the black wires from the connector and the second motor.

**6.** Hot glue two table tennis balls together. Repeat with the other two balls. Then glue both pairs together to make a square.

Some table tennis players can hit the ball at more than 100 miles (161 kilometers) per hour. Maybe try it before gluing yours together. But go outside first.

**7.** Cut off the rounded ends of both craft sticks. You should have two sticks about 3½ inches (9 cm) long.

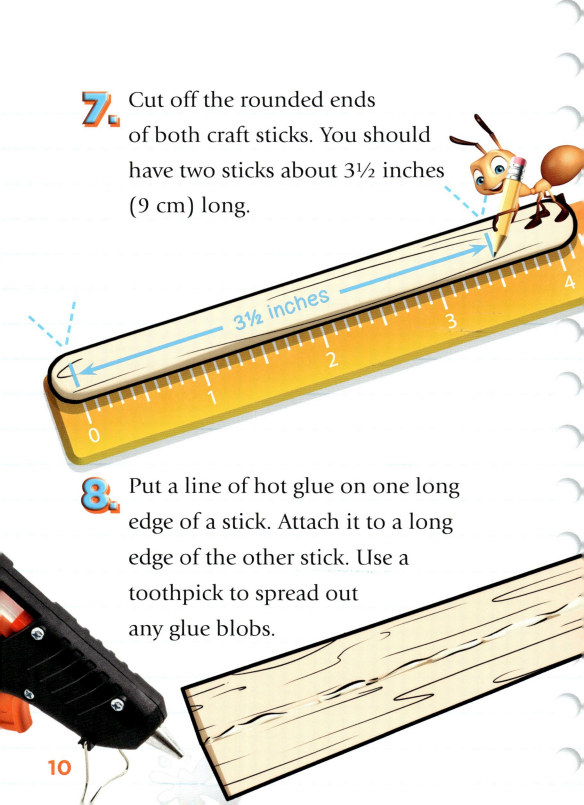

3½ inches

0  1  2  3  4

**8.** Put a line of hot glue on one long edge of a stick. Attach it to a long edge of the other stick. Use a toothpick to spread out any glue blobs.

**9.** Hot glue the sticks across the center of the balls.

11

battery

9V

terminals

**10.** Hot glue the battery to the craft sticks. Face the **terminals** to the center of the square of balls.

**11.** Hot glue the motor with the alligator clip to the top of the battery. Hang the shaft over the battery's back edge.

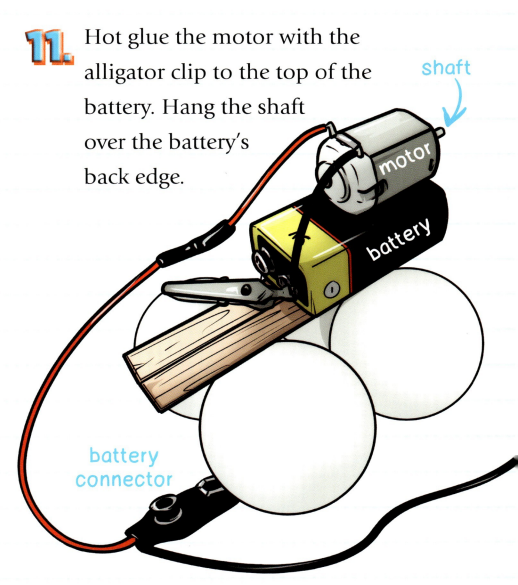

shaft

motor

battery

battery connector

**12.** Snap the battery connector on the battery.

**13.** Hot glue the other motor to the craft sticks. Hang the shaft over the edge of the sticks.

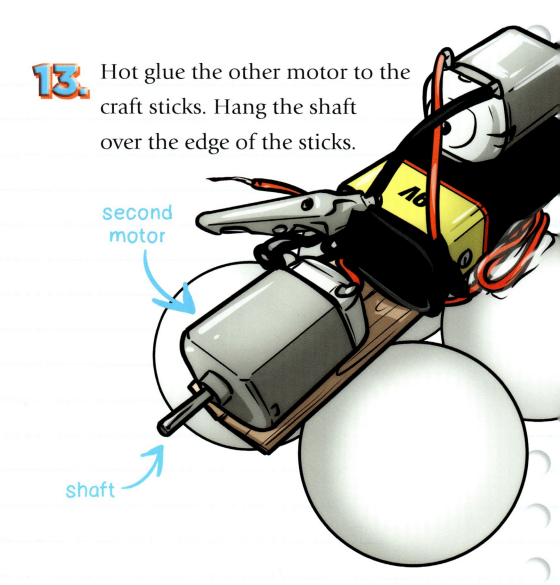

second motor

shaft

**14.** Clean up the wires. Fold them together and hot glue them to the balls. Make sure the alligator clip reaches the exposed red wire.

**15.** Cut off the top 2 inches (5 cm) of the water bottle.

2 inches

**16.** Cut flaps around the bottle piece. The flaps should be about 1 inch (3 cm) wide and 1½ inches (4 cm) deep.

1½ inches deep

1 inch wide

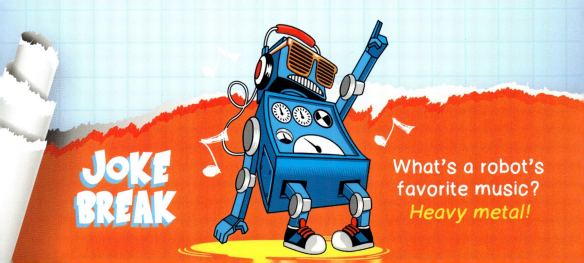

JOKE BREAK

What's a robot's favorite music?
*Heavy metal!*

**17.** Bend each flap up, at an **angle**, toward the lid of the bottle. When you let go of the flap, it should point out to the side.

**18.** Take the bottle cap off. Use a screwdriver to poke a hole in the center of the cap. Have an adult help with this part.

**19.** Put a small blob of hot glue on the shaft of the motor on the battery. Slide the bottle cap onto the shaft. Face the top of the cap toward the battery. Put more glue on the inside of the bottle cap where the shaft sticks through.

**20.** Screw the cut plastic bottle back on the cap.

**21.** Cut a ½-inch (1-cm) cube from the eraser. Use a pencil to poke a hole in the eraser. The hole should be a little off-center. Slide the eraser onto the shaft of the second motor. Hot glue the eraser to the shaft.

motor

battery

bottle cap

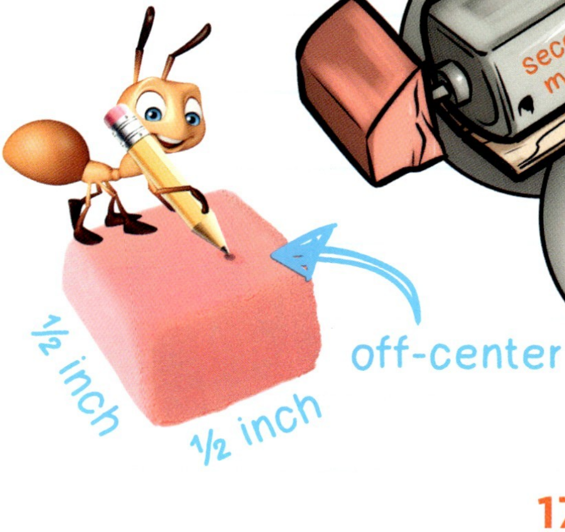

second motor

½ inch

½ inch

off-center

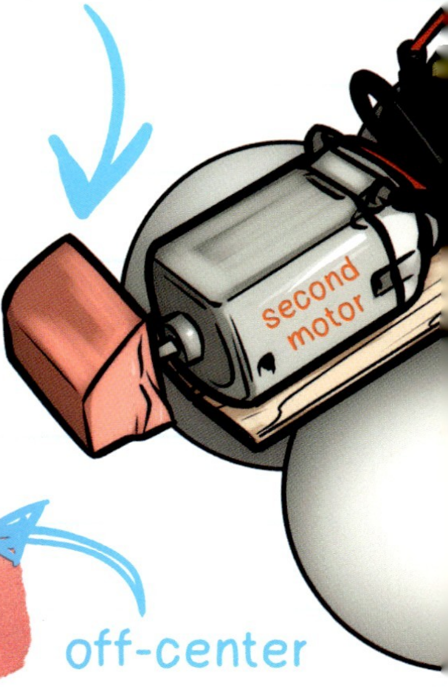

**22.** Make your robot go crazy. Clamp the alligator clip to the exposed red wire. The robot should **vibrate** while the fan spins. Watch your simple bot move across the table!

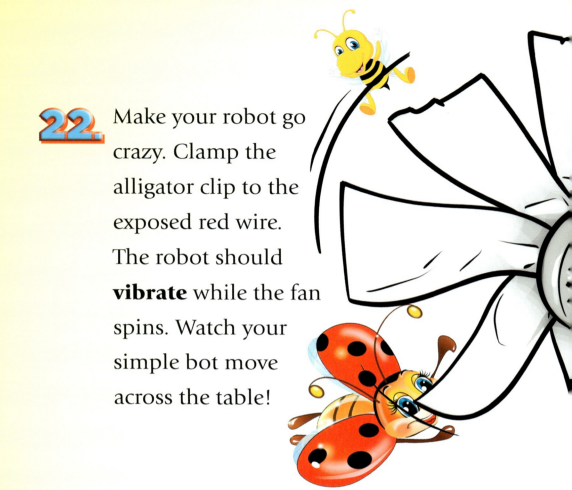

# Chapter 3
# GET IN ON THE HI JINX

**Engineers** are doing amazing things with robots. Some bots battle in rings. Others save people's lives. Now you have some skills to create your own robots. How will you get in on the fun?

# Take It One Step More

1. Bend the fan blades a different way. Can you get the bot to go backward?

2. What could you use in place of table tennis balls?

3. How could you build on this design? Is there a way to make this robot start and stop on its own?

# GLOSSARY

**angle** (AYN-gul)—the space or shape formed when two lines or surfaces meet

**clamp** (KLAMP)—to hold tightly

**engineer** (en-juh-NEER)—a designer or builder

**exposed** (ek-SPOZD)—not covered

**shaft** (SHAFT)—a cylindrical bar used to support rotating pieces

**terminal** (TUR-muh-nuhl)—a device attached to the end of a wire, cable, or electrical device to make connections

**vibrate** (VI-brayt)—to swing or move to and fro

## BOOKS

**Chow-Miller, Ian.** *Sensors and the Environment.* Robotics. New York: Cavendish Square Publishing, 2017.

**Cunningham, Kevin.** *Robot Scientist.* Cool STEAM Careers. Ann Arbor, MI: Cherry Lake Publishing, 2016.

**Murphy, Maggie.** *High-Tech DIY Projects with Robotics.* Maker Kids. New York: PowerKids Press, 2015.

## WEBSITES

Build Your First Robot
**www.popularmechanics.com/technology/robots/a7388/build-your-first-robot/**

History of Robotics: Timeline
**www.robotshop.com/media/files/PDF/timeline.pdf**

Robotics: Facts
**idahoptv.org/sciencetrek/topics/robots/facts.cfm**

Adults are boring. But they can be really helpful. Don't be afraid to ask for help if you get stuck.

If your wires don't have exposed ends, don't worry. Use a wire stripper to take off as much of the wire casing as needed. (See first tip.)

Try using different sizes of eraser to see which one works best. You could also try using a different material, such as cork.

The author is super cool. He made a short video of his crazy car bot. Check it out on Black Rabbit Books' YouTube channel.